Richard
STRAUSS

SERENADE
IN E-FLAT MAJOR
Op.7
Edited by
Richard W. Sargeant, Jr.

Study Score
Partitur

SERENISSIMA MUSIC, INC.

ORCHESTRA

2 Flutes

2 Oboes

2 Clarinets (B-flat)

2 Bassoons

Contrabassoon

4 Horns (F)*

*The present score has been updated for the common keys of modern instruments
(Clarinets in A or B-flat, Horns in F, Trumpets in C). The composer's original score featured
Horns in E-flat (1 and 2), B-flat basso (3 and 4).

Duration: ca. 10 minutes

Premiere: November 27, 1882
Dresden, German Empire
Court Theatre
Court Orchestra Ensemble / Franz Wüllner

ISMN: 979-0-58042-119-7
This score is a newly engraved urtext edition prepared
from the primary sources.

Printed in the USA
First Printing: September, 2018

SERENADE IN E-FLAT MAJOR

OP.7

Richard Strauss
Edited by Richard W. Sargeant, Jr.

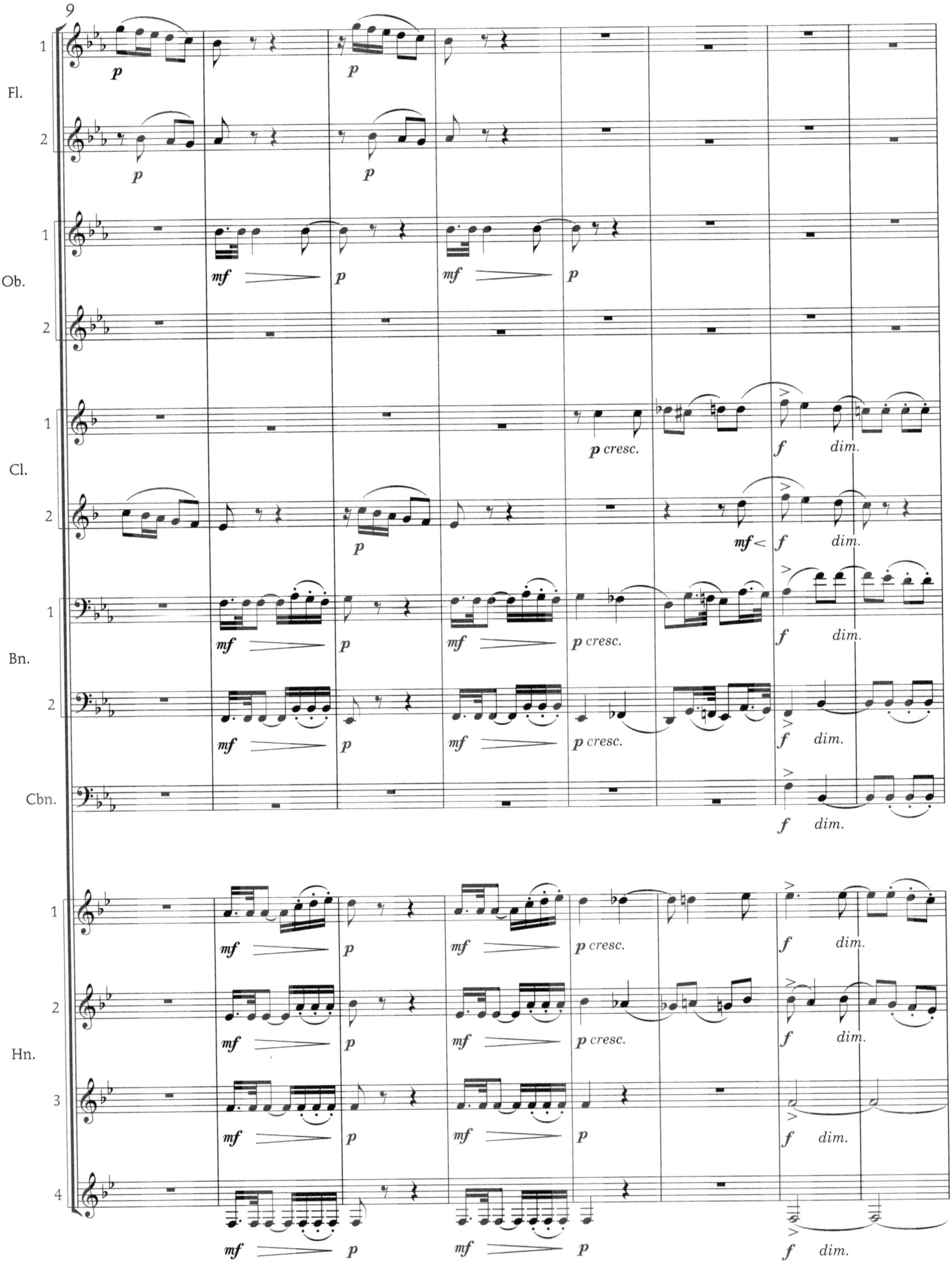
9
Fl.
1
2
Ob.
1
2
Cl.
1
2
Bn.
1
2
Cbn.
Hn.
1
2
3
4
p
mf
p cresc.
f
dim.
mf<

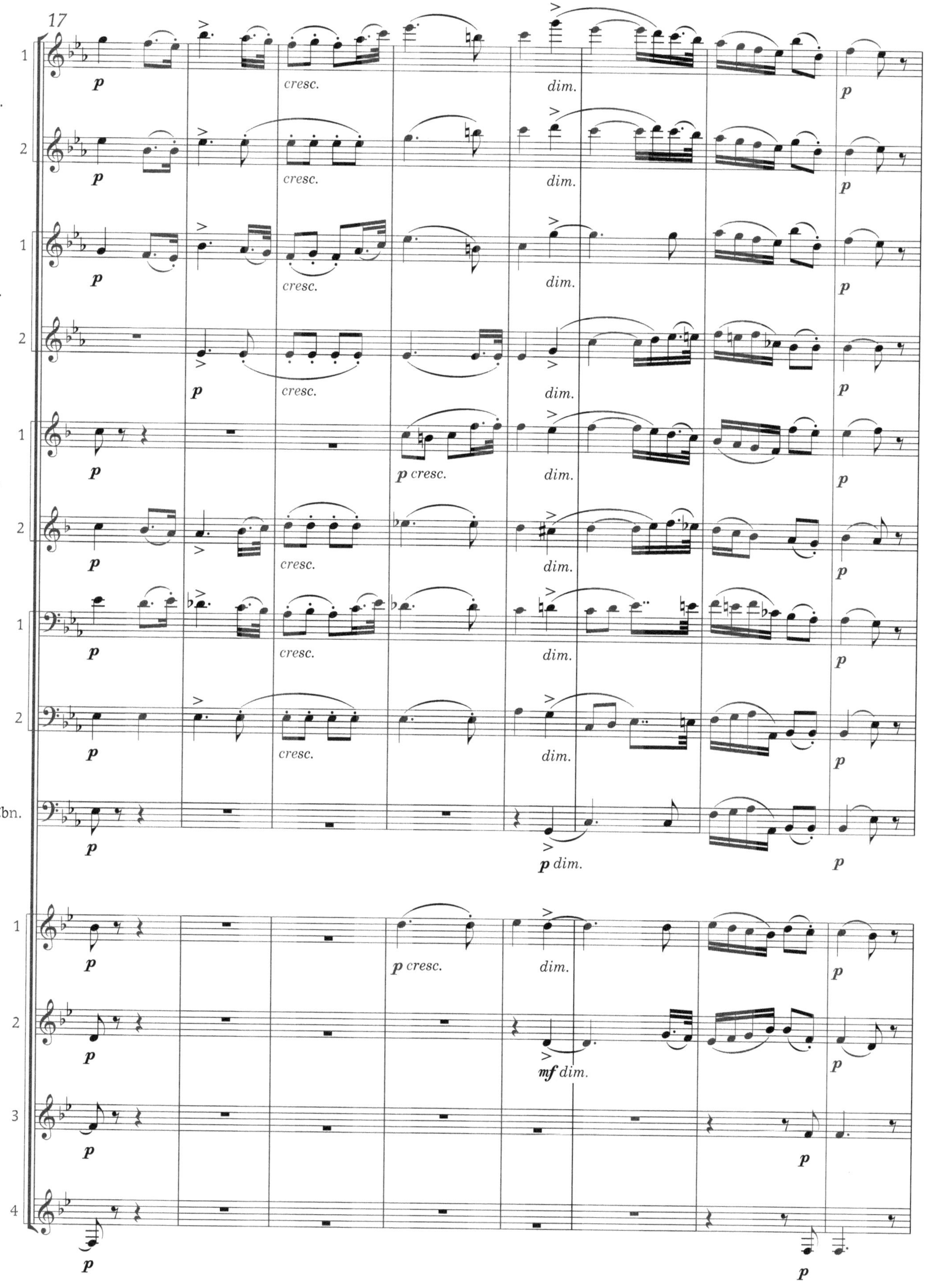
17
Fl.
Ob.
Cl.
Bn.
Cbn.
Hn.
p
cresc.
dim.
p cresc.
p dim.
mf dim.

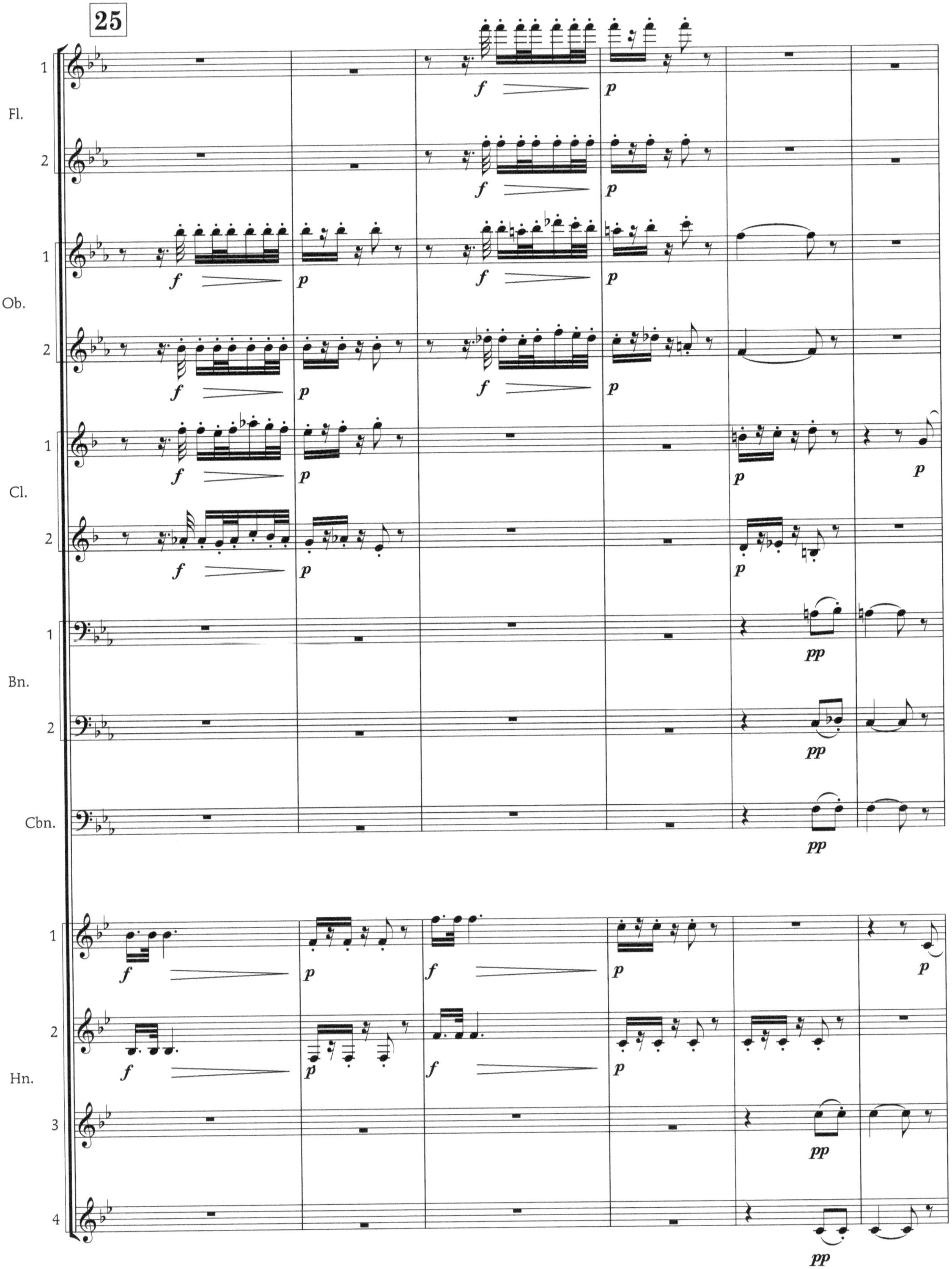
25
Fl.
Ob.
Cl.
Bn.
Cbn.
Hn.

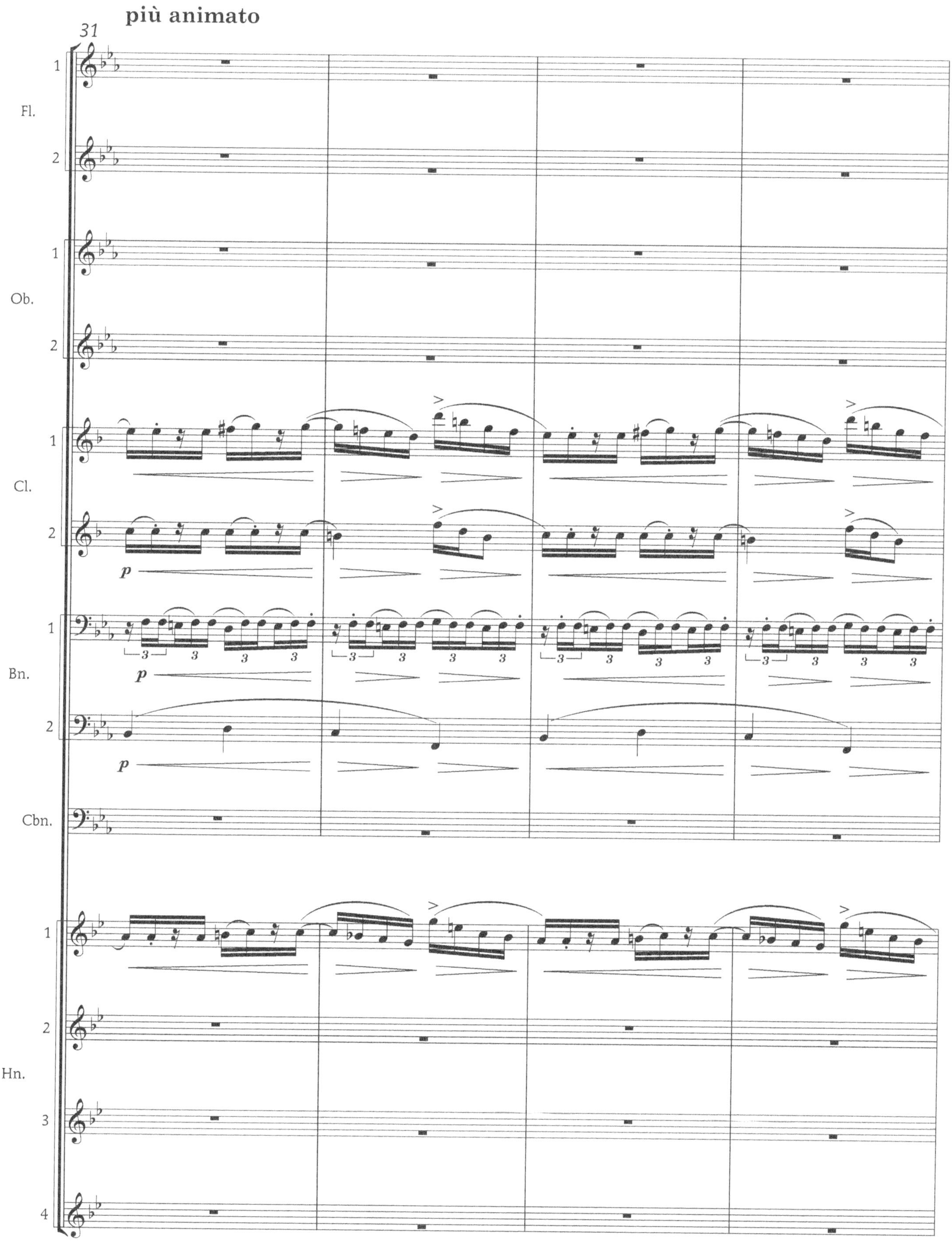
più animato
31
Fl.
Ob.
Cl.
Bn.
Cbn.
Hn.
p

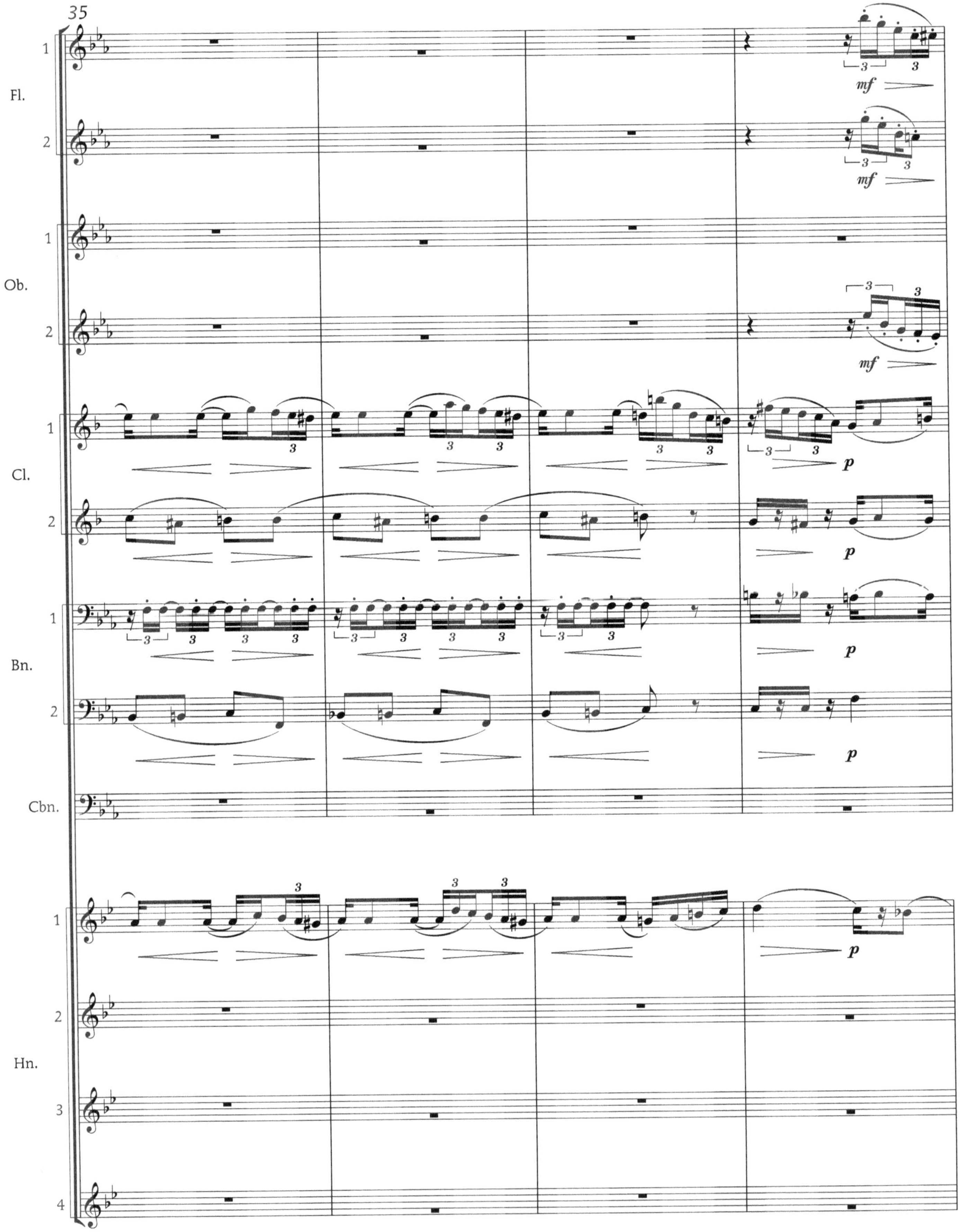
35
Fl.
Ob.
Cl.
Bn.
Cbn.
Hn.
mf
p

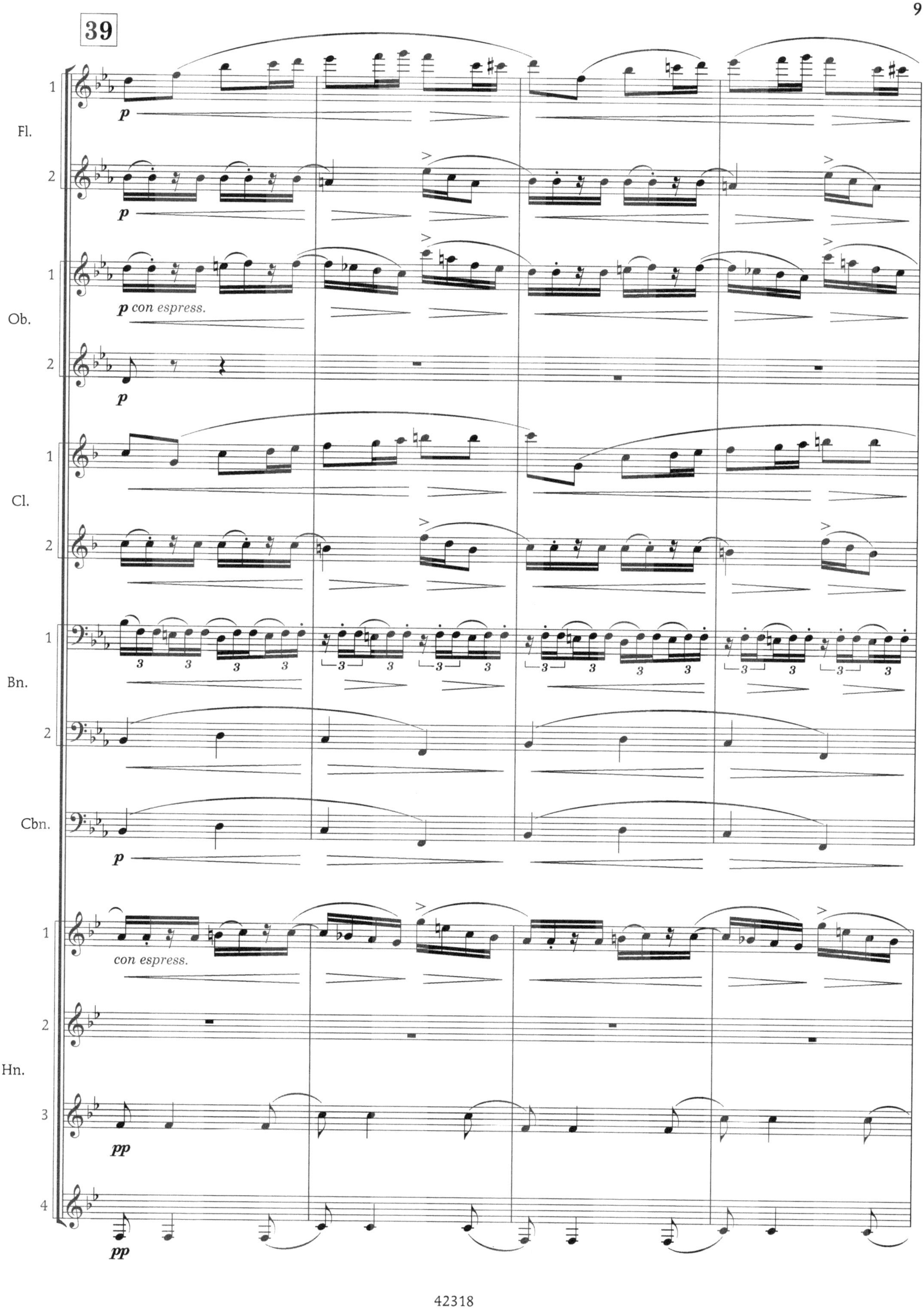
39
Fl.
1
2
p
Ob.
p con espress.
Cl.
Bn.
3
Cbn.
Hn.
4
con espress.
pp

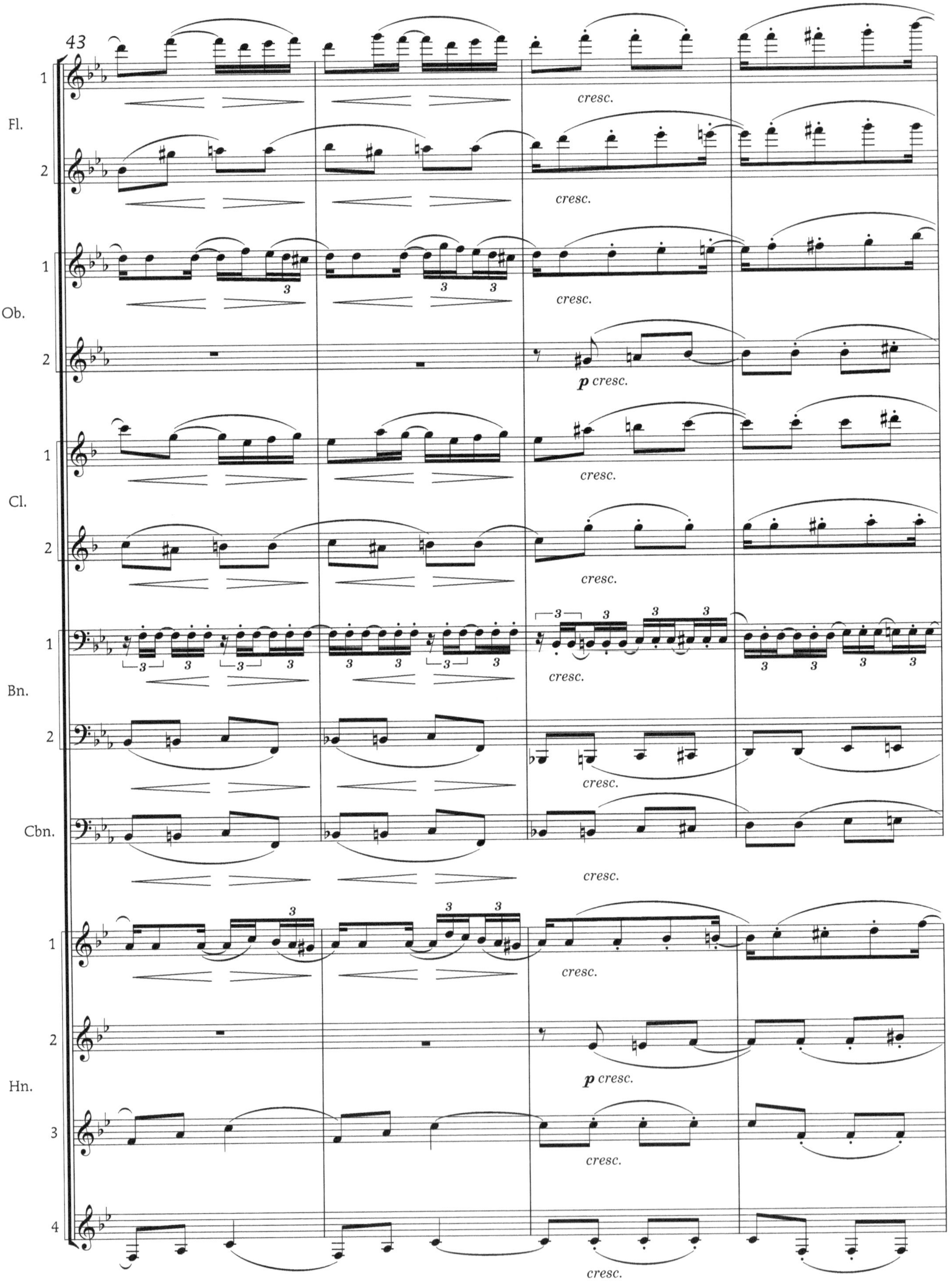
43
Fl.
1
2
Ob.
1
2
Cl.
1
2
Bn.
1
2
Cbn.
Hn.
1
2
3
4
cresc.
p cresc.
3

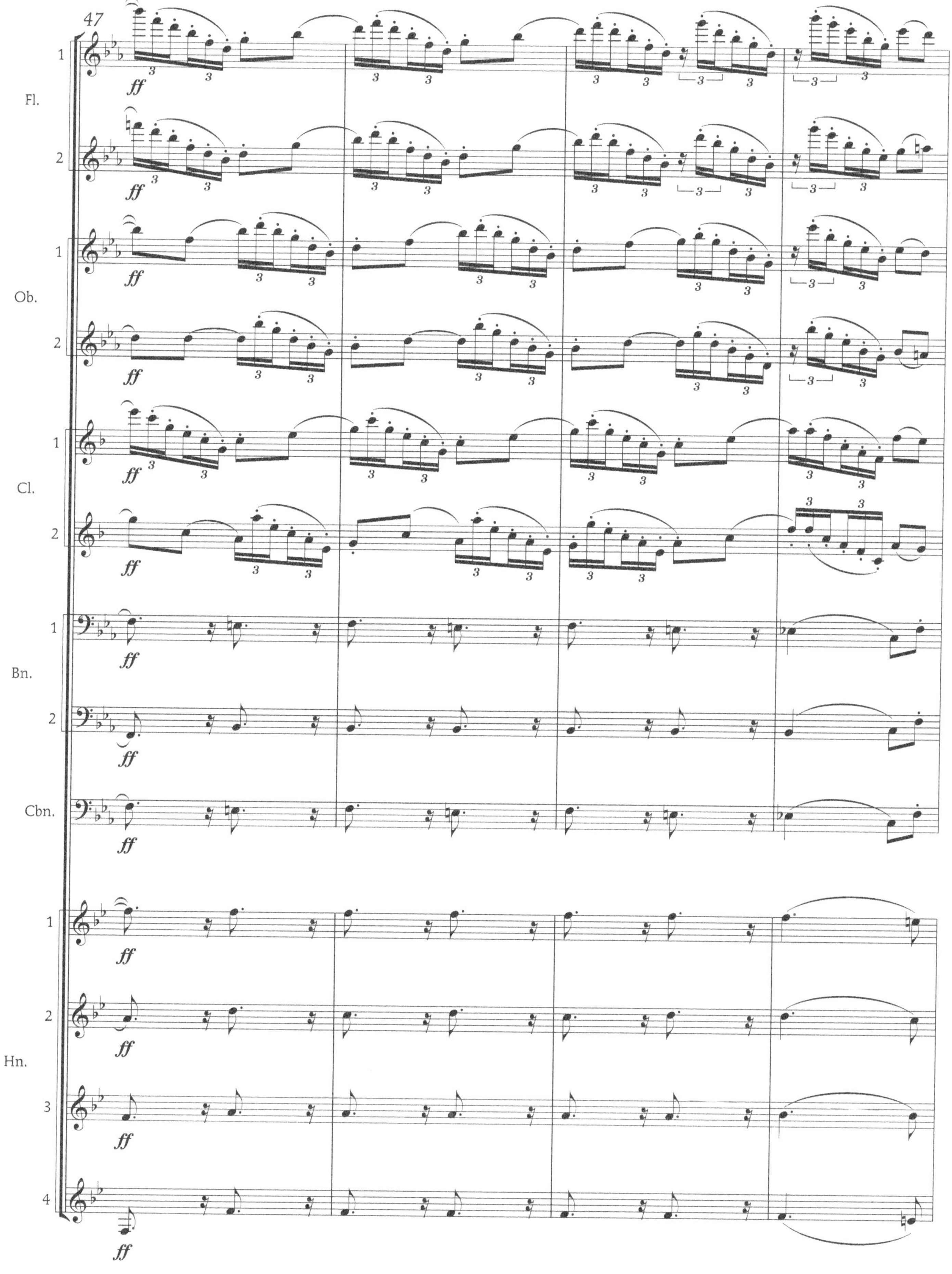
47
Fl.
Ob.
Cl.
Bn.
Cbn.
Hn.
ff

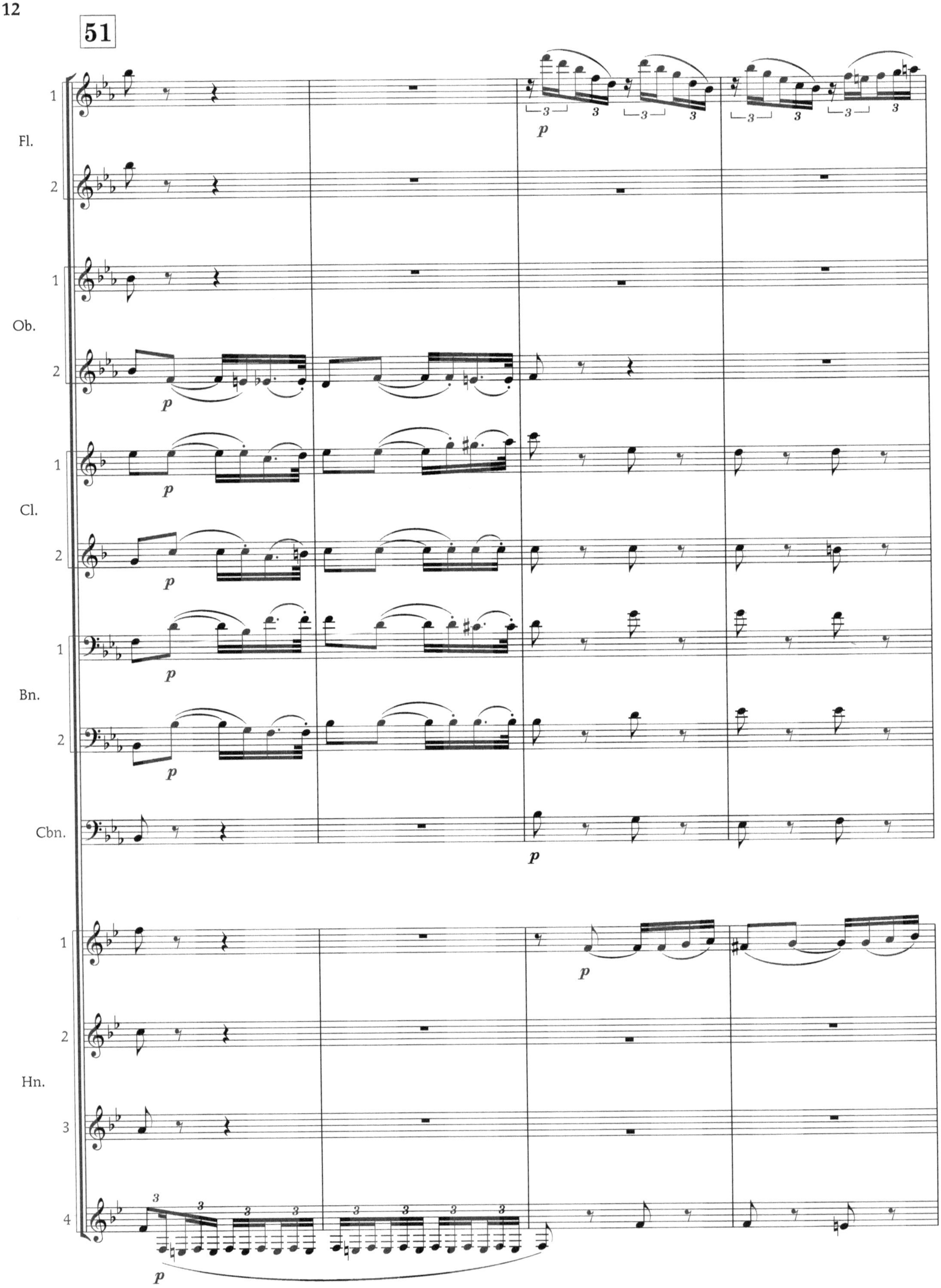
51
Fl.
1
2
Ob.
1
2
Cl.
1
2
Bn.
1
2
Cbn.
Hn.
1
2
3
4
p

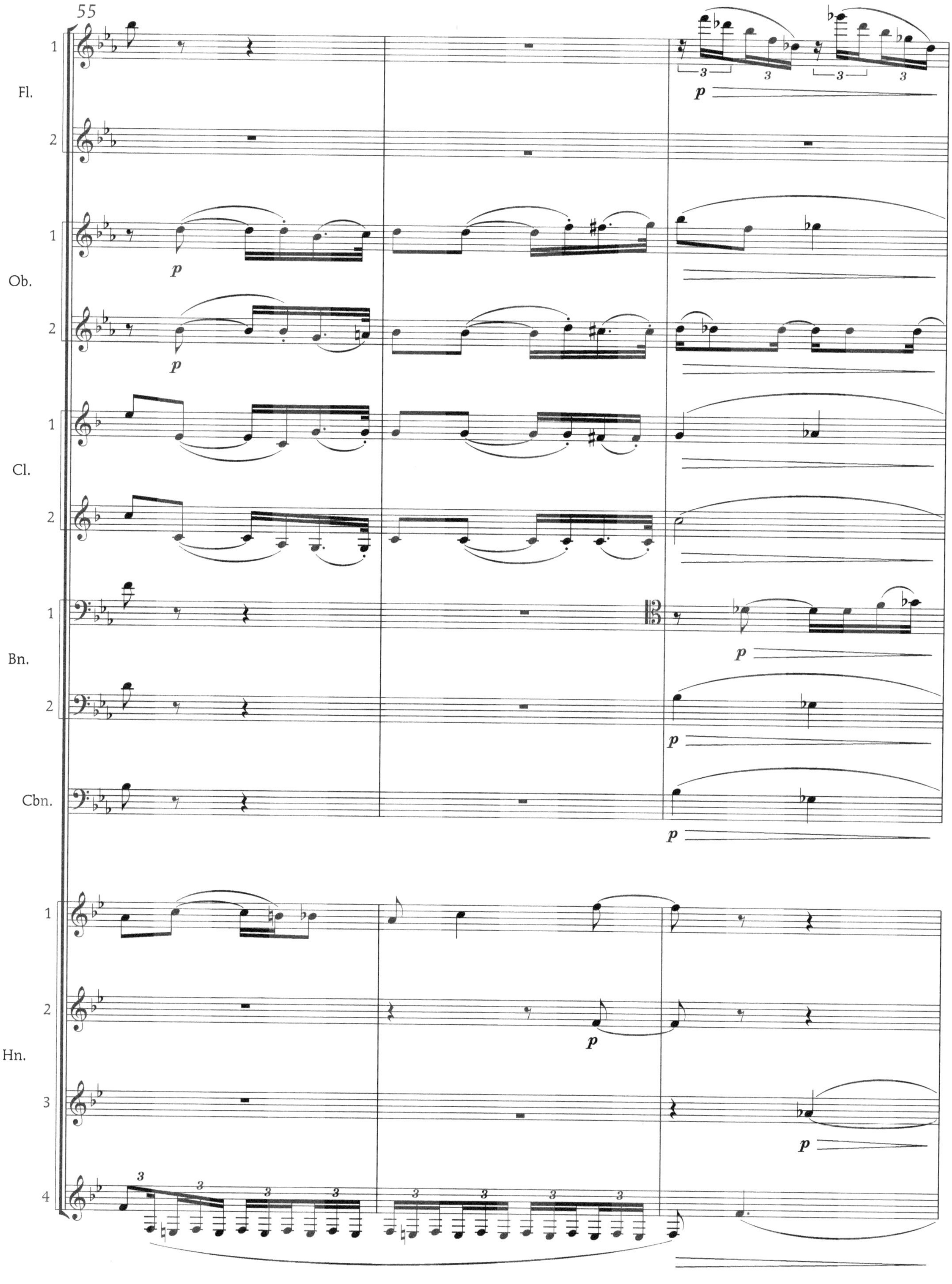
55
Fl.
Ob.
Cl.
Bn.
Cbn.
Hn.
p

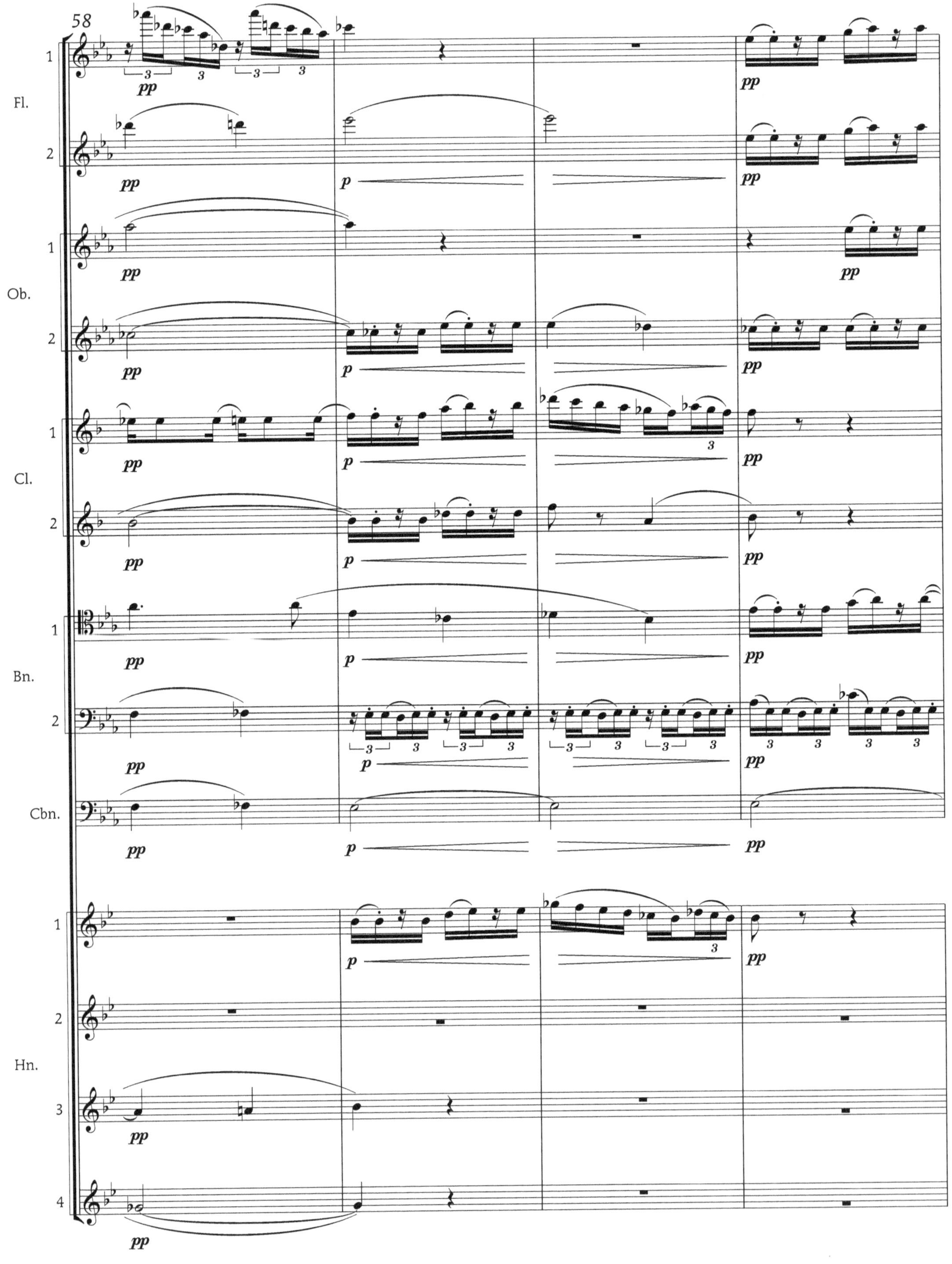
58
Fl.
Ob.
Cl.
Bn.
Cbn.
Hn.
pp
p

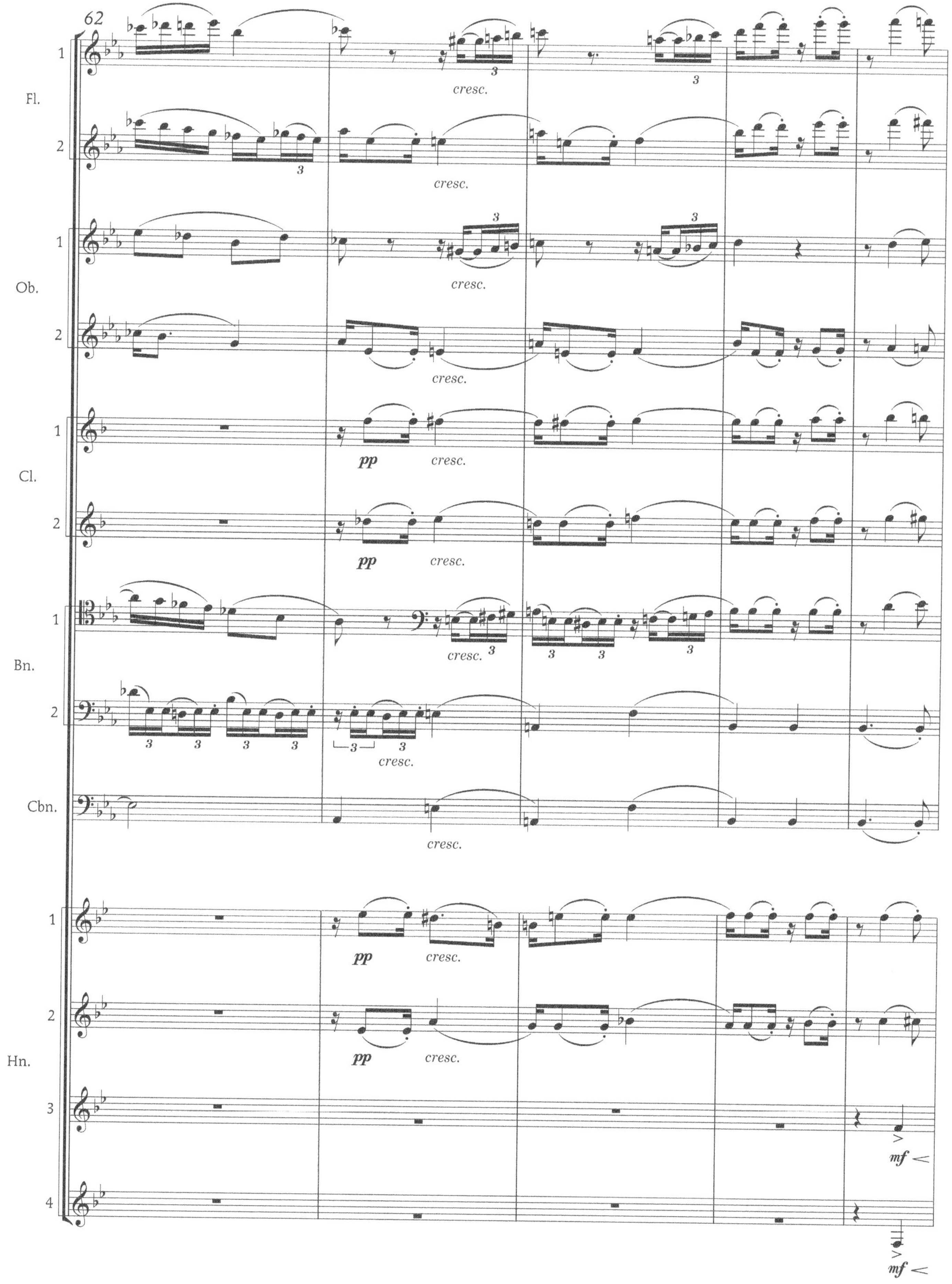
62
Fl.
Ob.
Cl.
Bn.
Cbn.
Hn.
cresc.
pp
mf

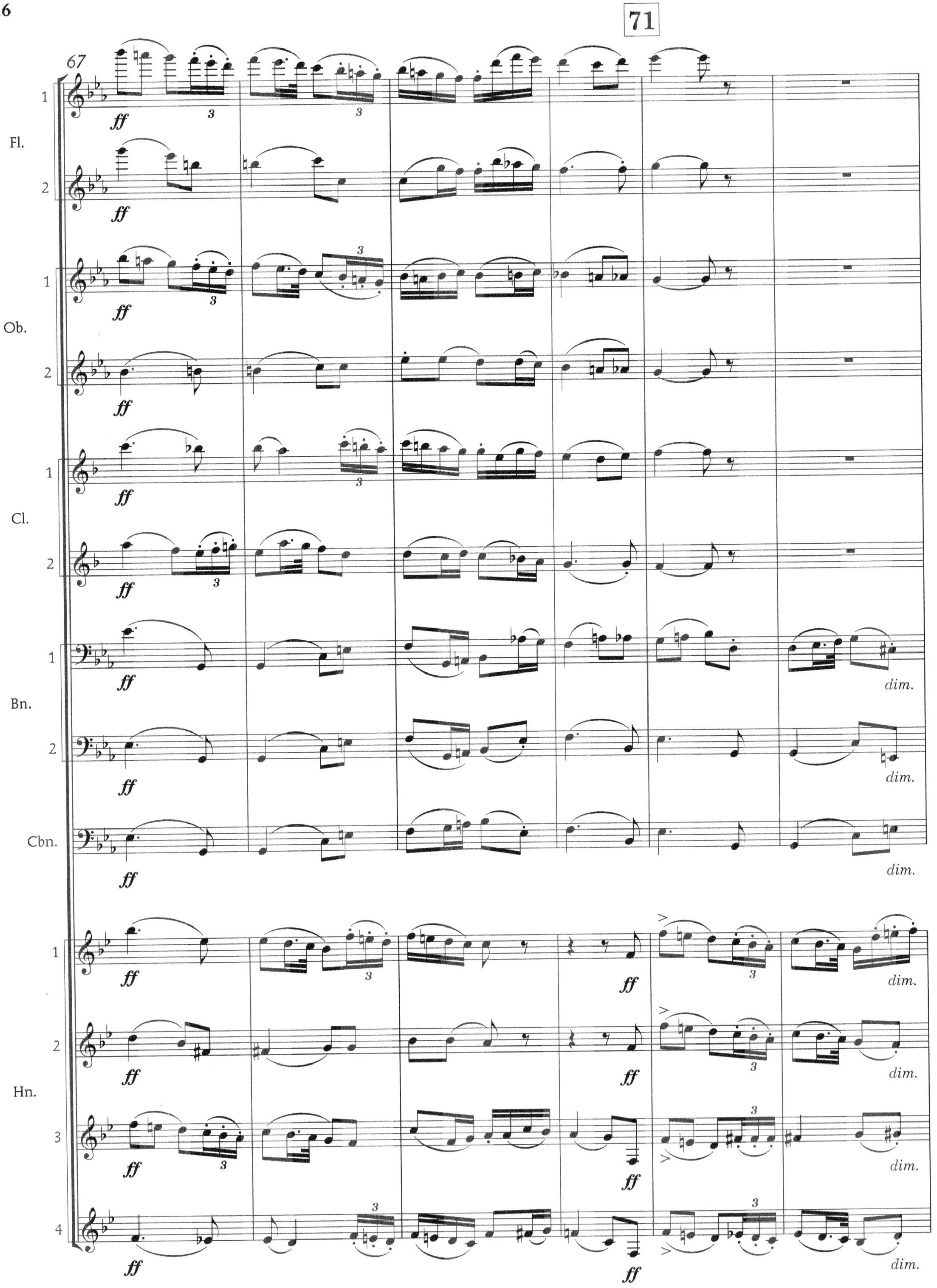
71
67
Fl.
Ob.
Cl.
Bn.
Cbn.
Hn.
ff
dim.

calando

Tempo I
80
Fl.
1
2
sostenuto
sostenuto
Ob.
1
2
pp sostenuto con espress.
Cl.
1
2
sostenuto
sostenuto
Bn.
1
2
sostenuto
Cbn.
sostenuto
Hn.
1
2
3
4
pp sostenuto
pp sostenuto
sostenuto
sostenuto

più animato

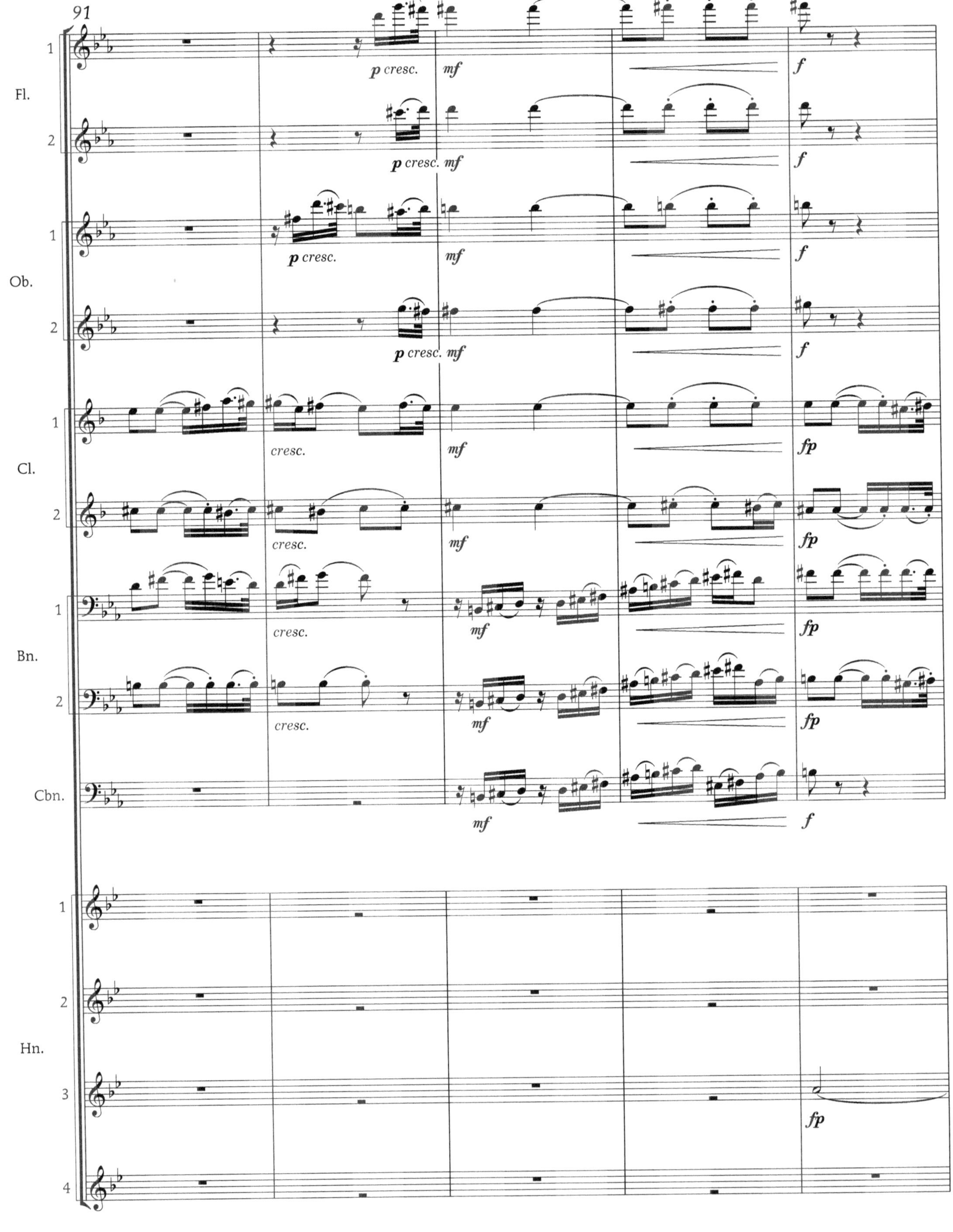
91
Fl.
Ob.
Cl.
Bn.
Cbn.
Hn.
p cresc.
mf
f
cresc.
fp

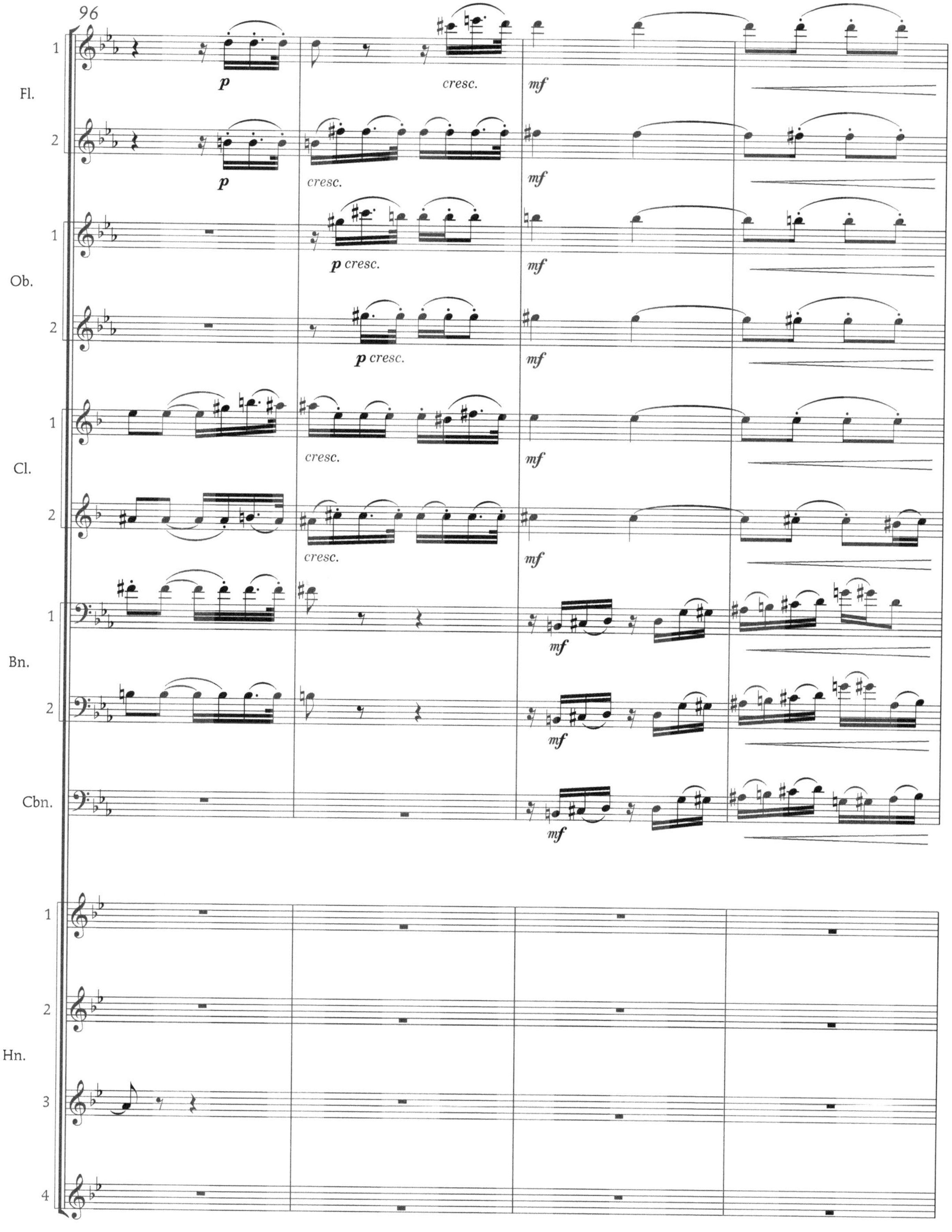
96
Fl.
Ob.
Cl.
Bn.
Cbn.
Hn.
p
cresc.
mf
p cresc.

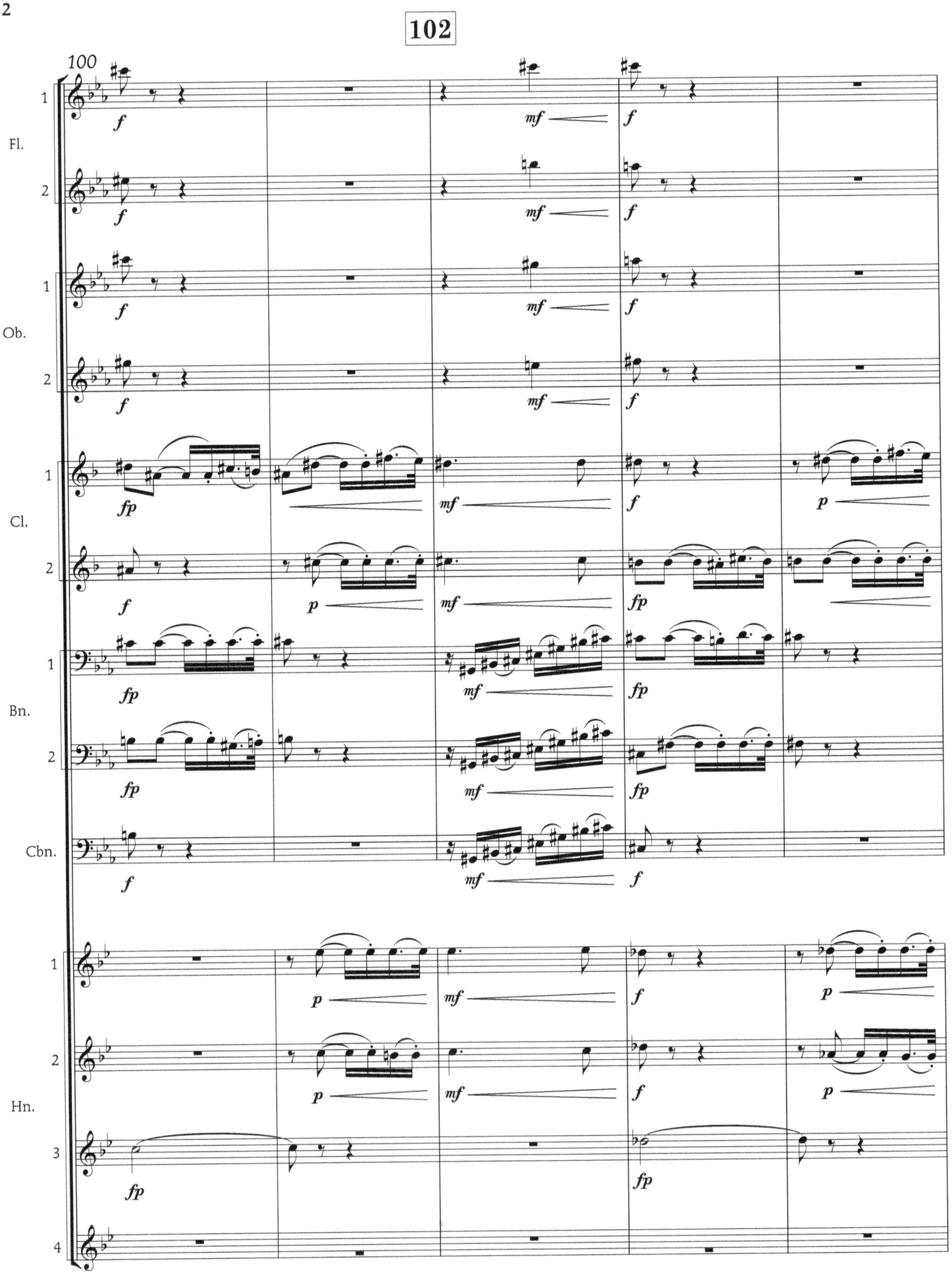
102
100
Fl.
Ob.
Cl.
Bn.
Cbn.
Hn.

string.

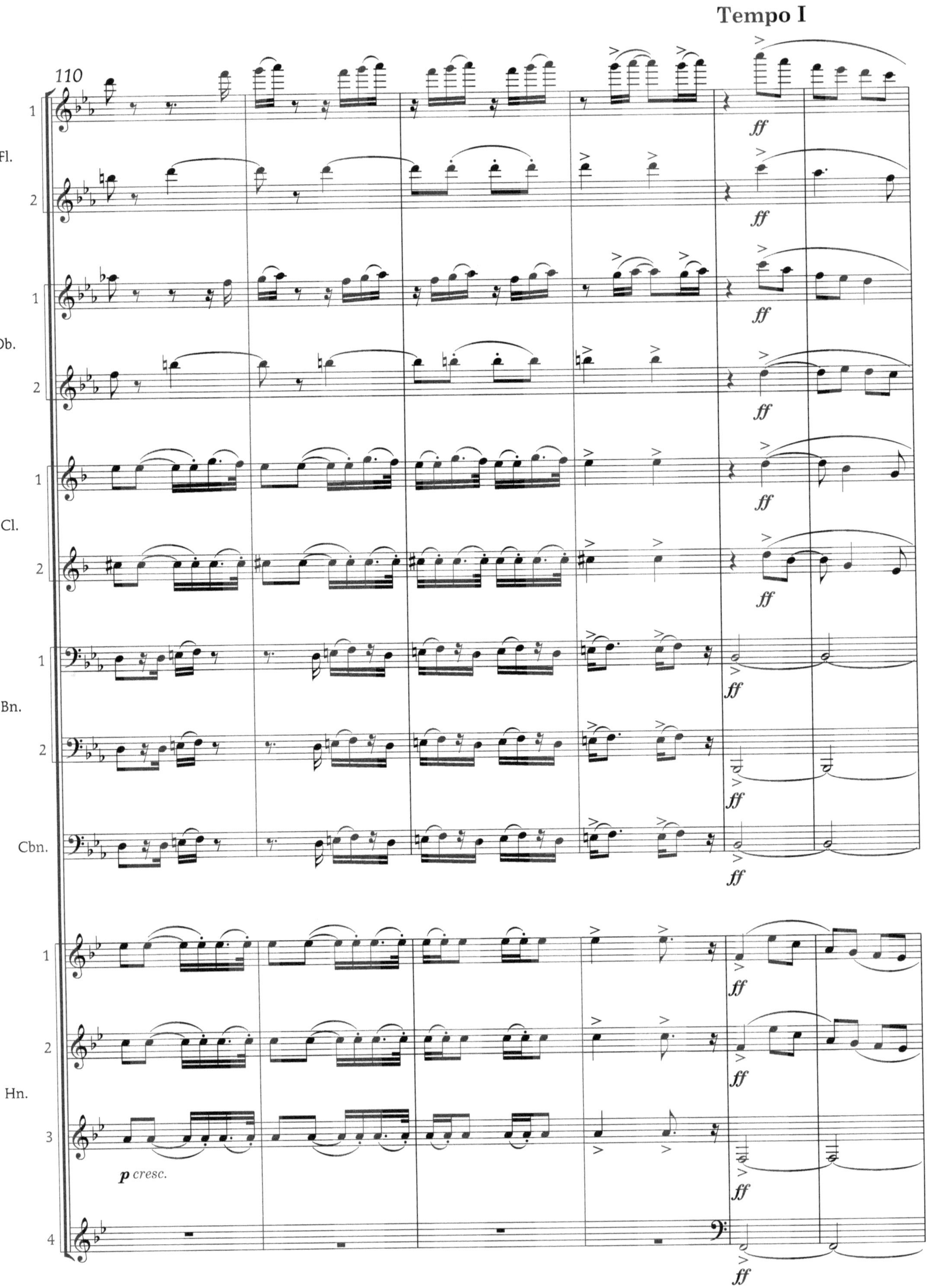
Tempo I
110
Fl.
Ob.
Cl.
Bn.
Cbn.
Hn.
ff
p cresc.

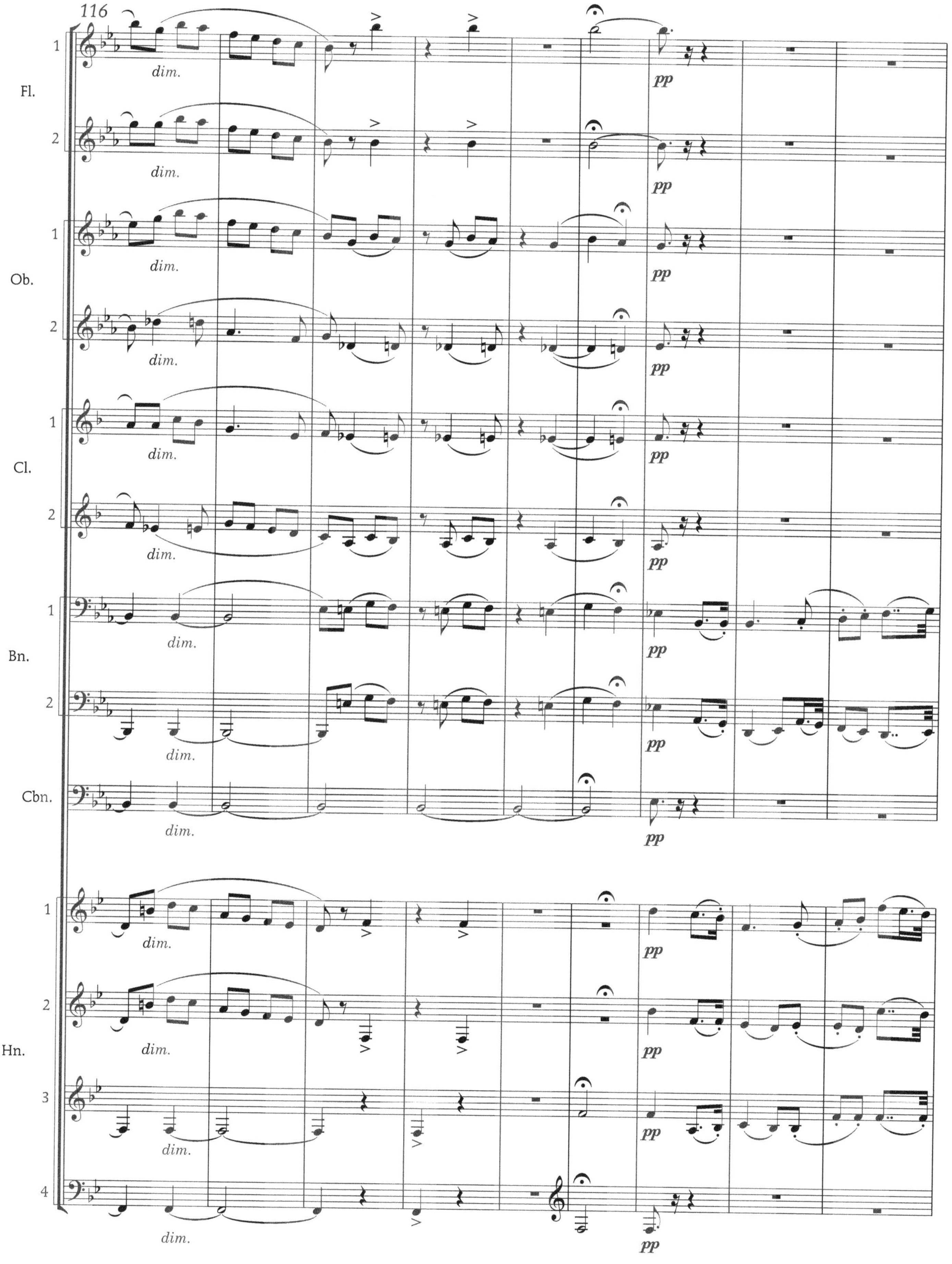
116
Fl.
Ob.
Cl.
Bn.
Cbn.
Hn.
dim.
pp

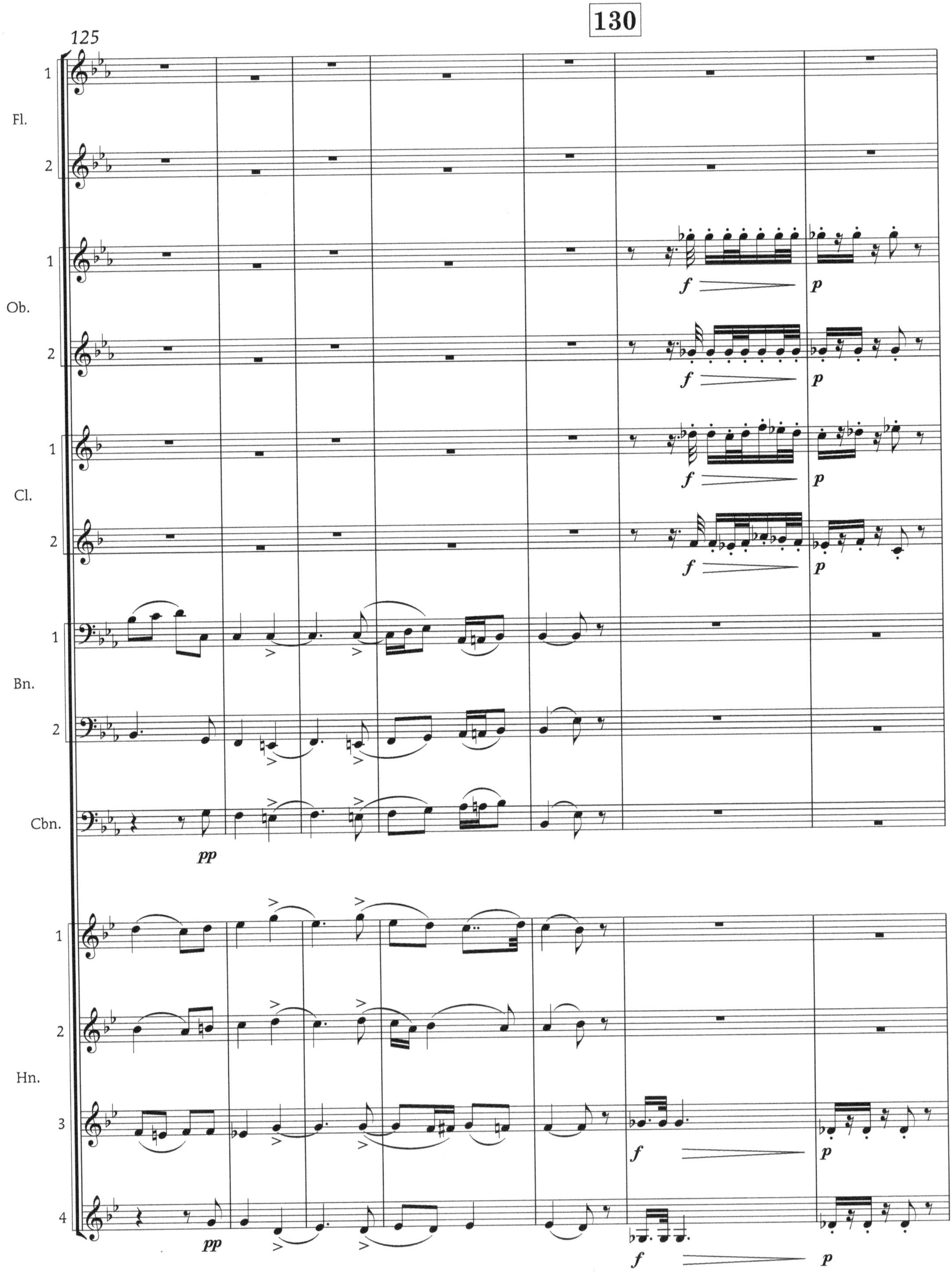
130
125
Fl.
Ob.
Cl.
Bn.
Cbn.
Hn.
f
p
pp

più animato

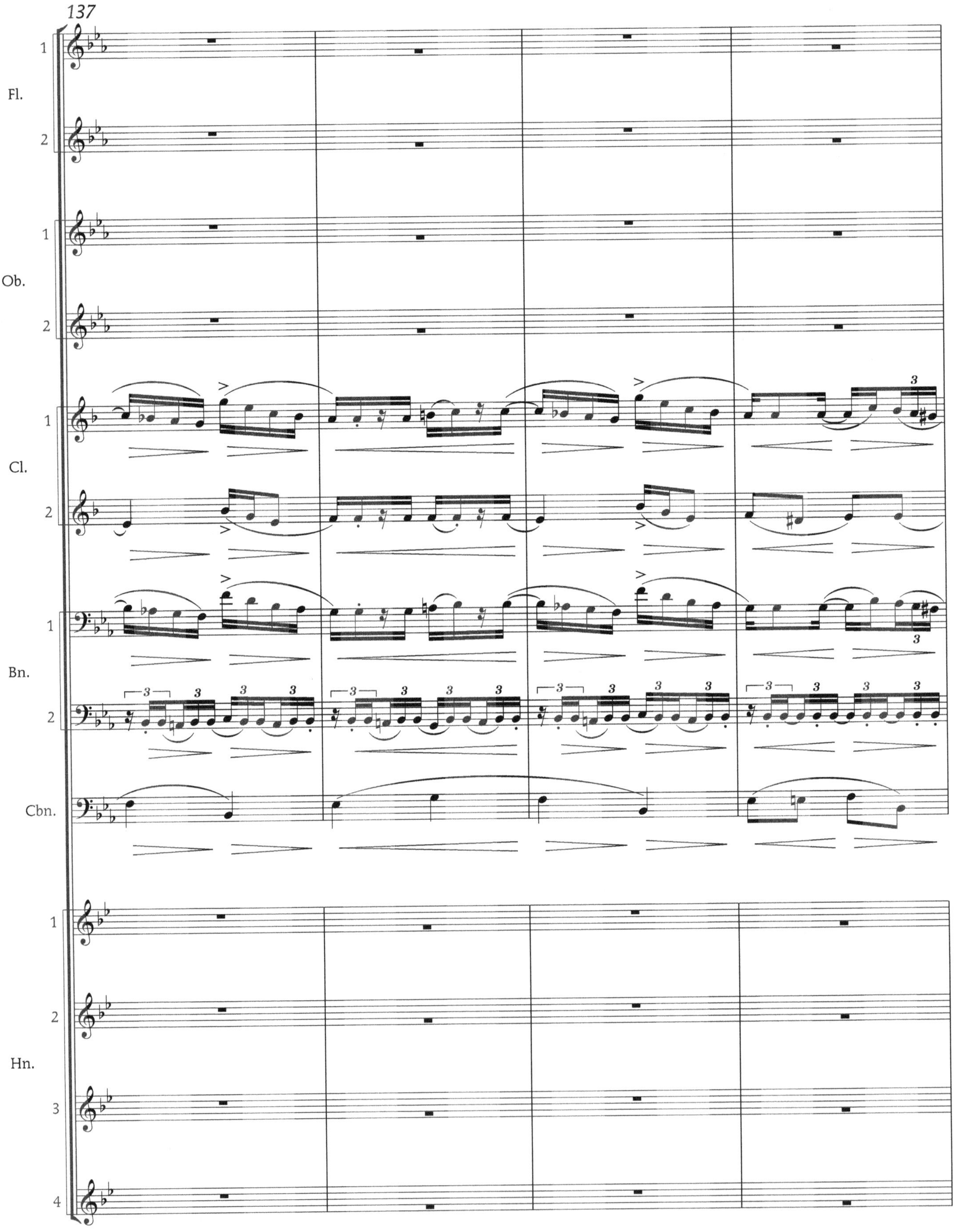
137
Fl.
1
2
Ob.
1
2
Cl.
1
2
Bn.
1
2
Cbn.
Hn.
1
2
3
4

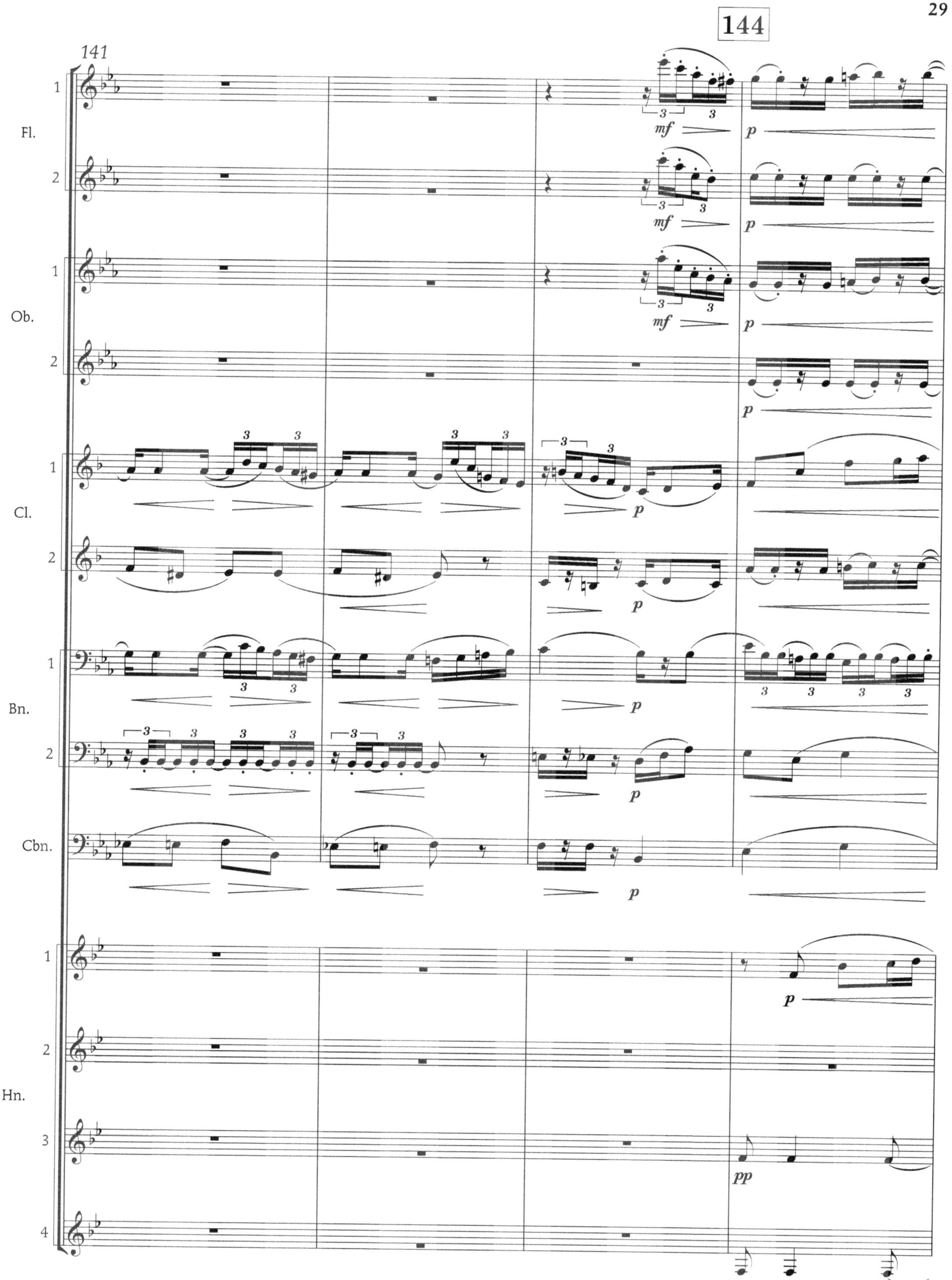
144
141
Fl.
Ob.
Cl.
Bn.
Cbn.
Hn.
mf
p
pp

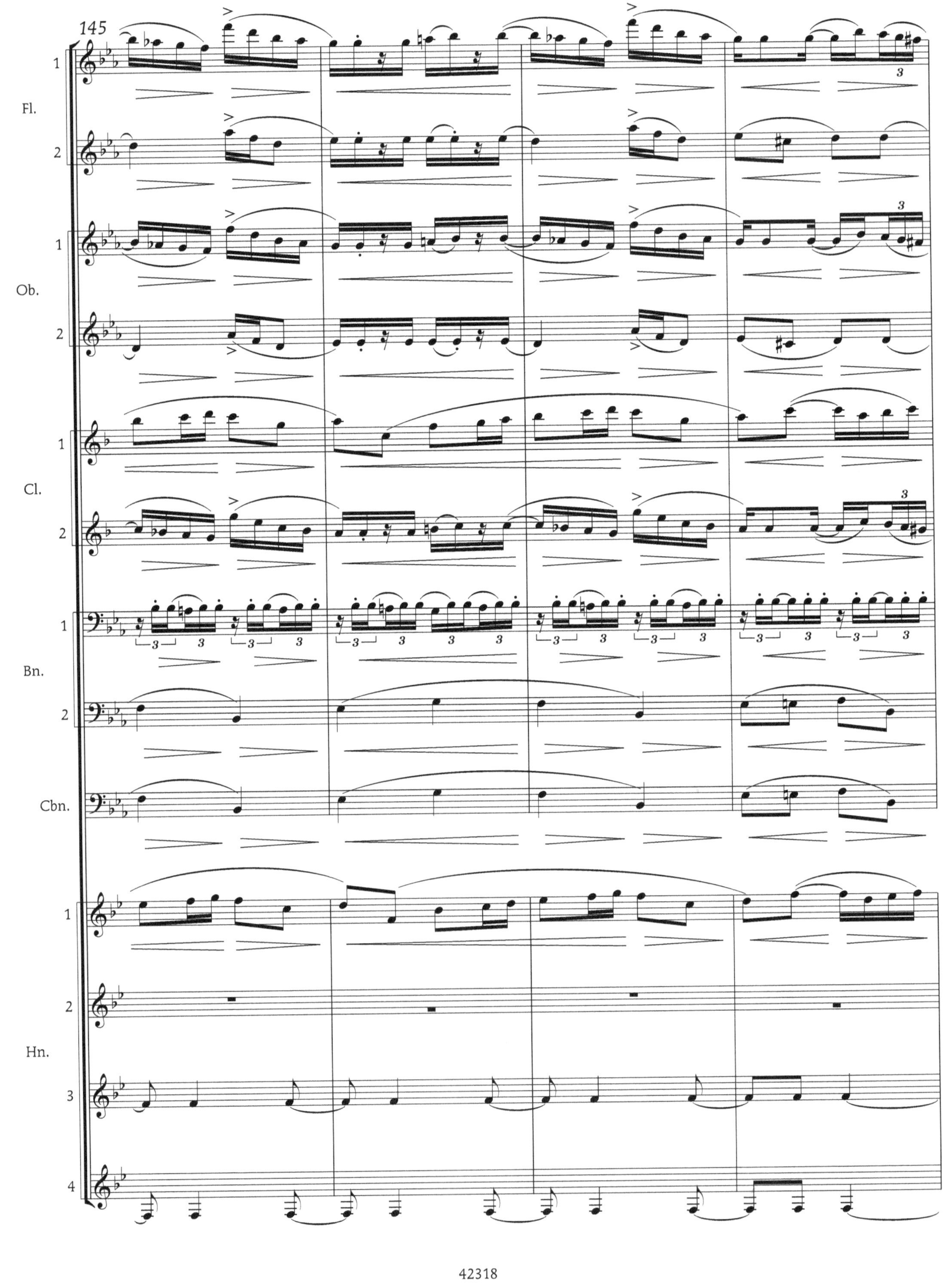
145
Fl.
1
2
Ob.
1
2
Cl.
1
2
Bn.
1
2
Cbn.
Hn.
1
2
3
4

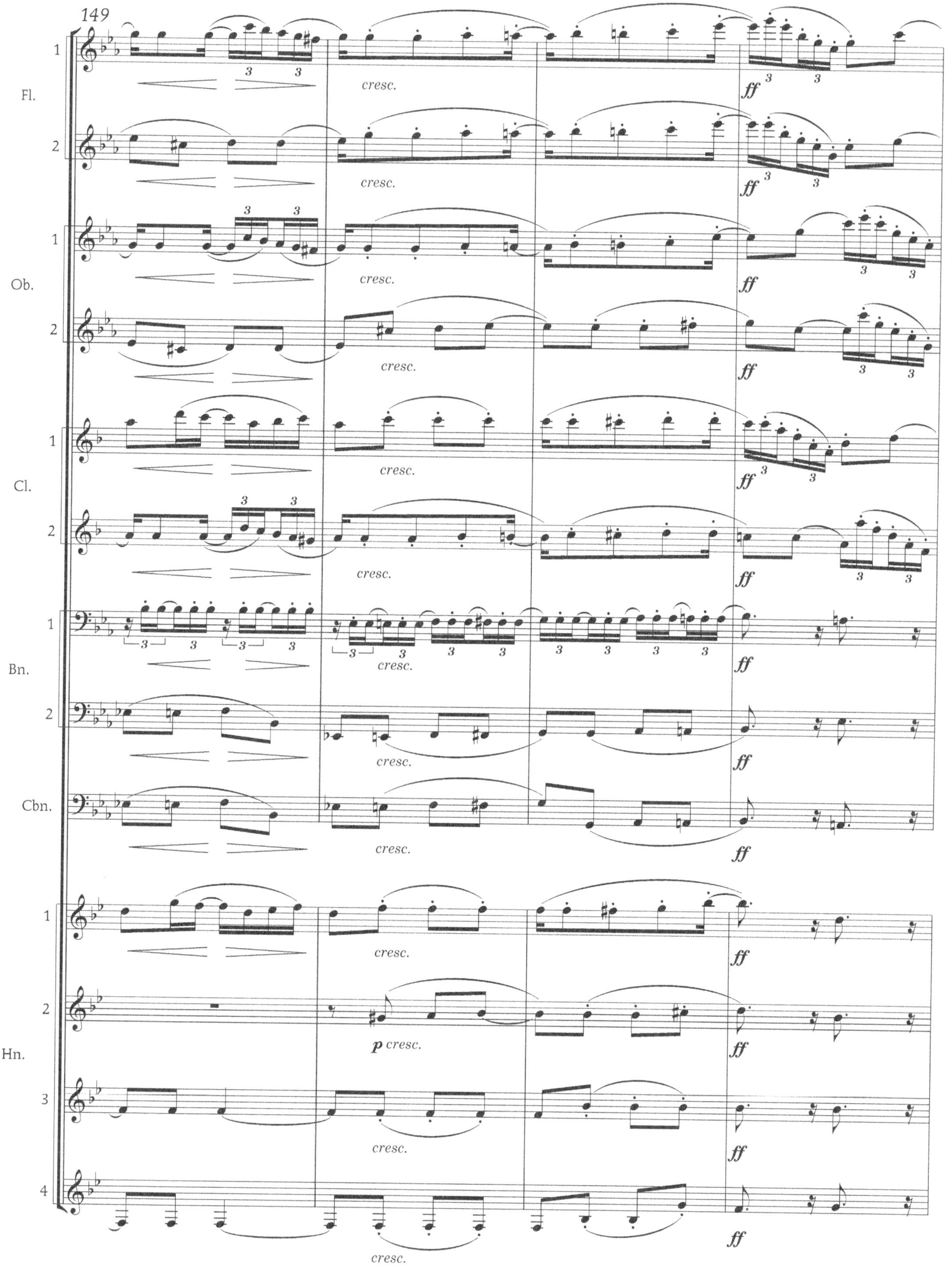
149
Fl.
Ob.
Cl.
Bn.
Cbn.
Hn.
cresc.
ff
p cresc.

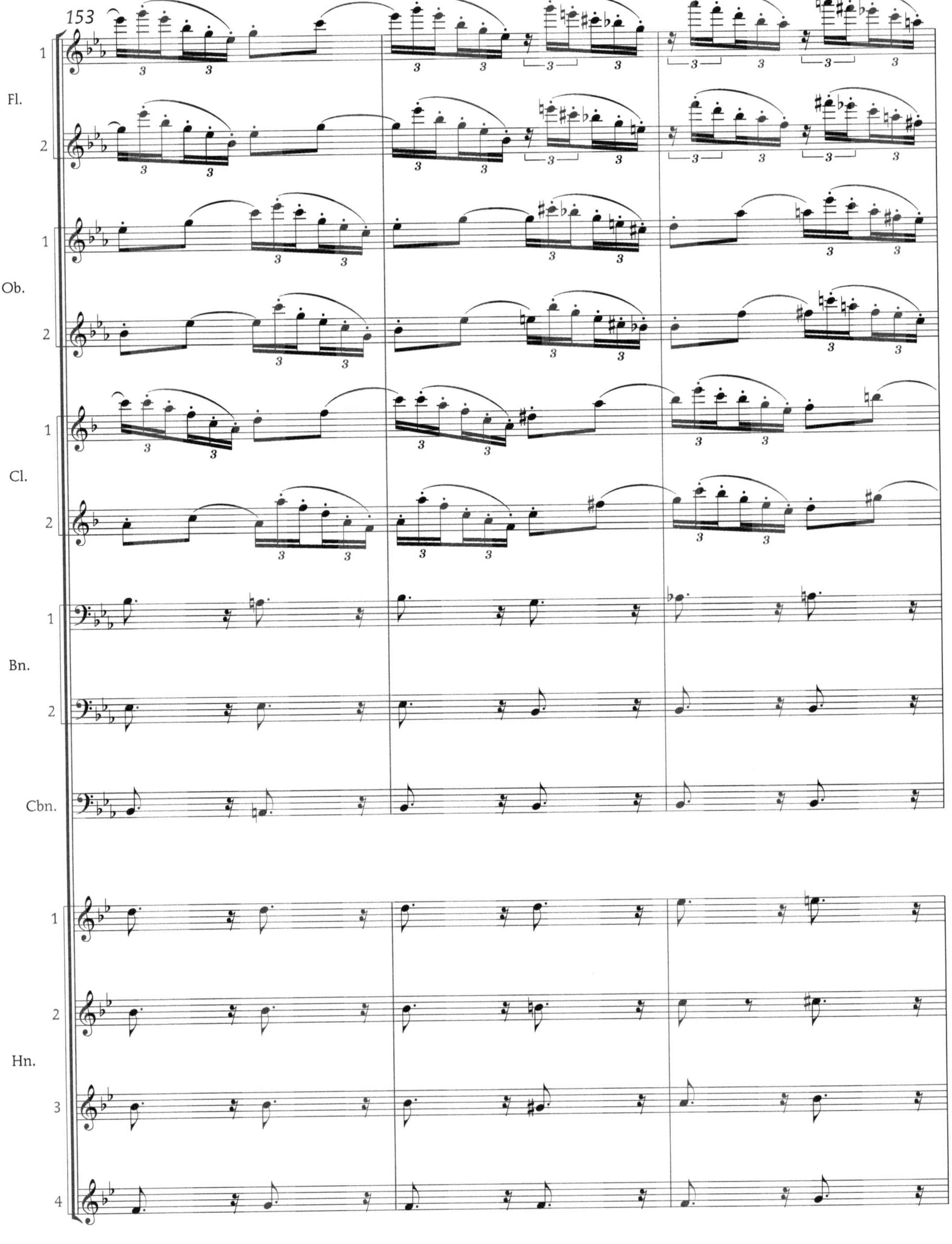
153
Fl.
Ob.
Cl.
Bn.
Cbn.
Hn.

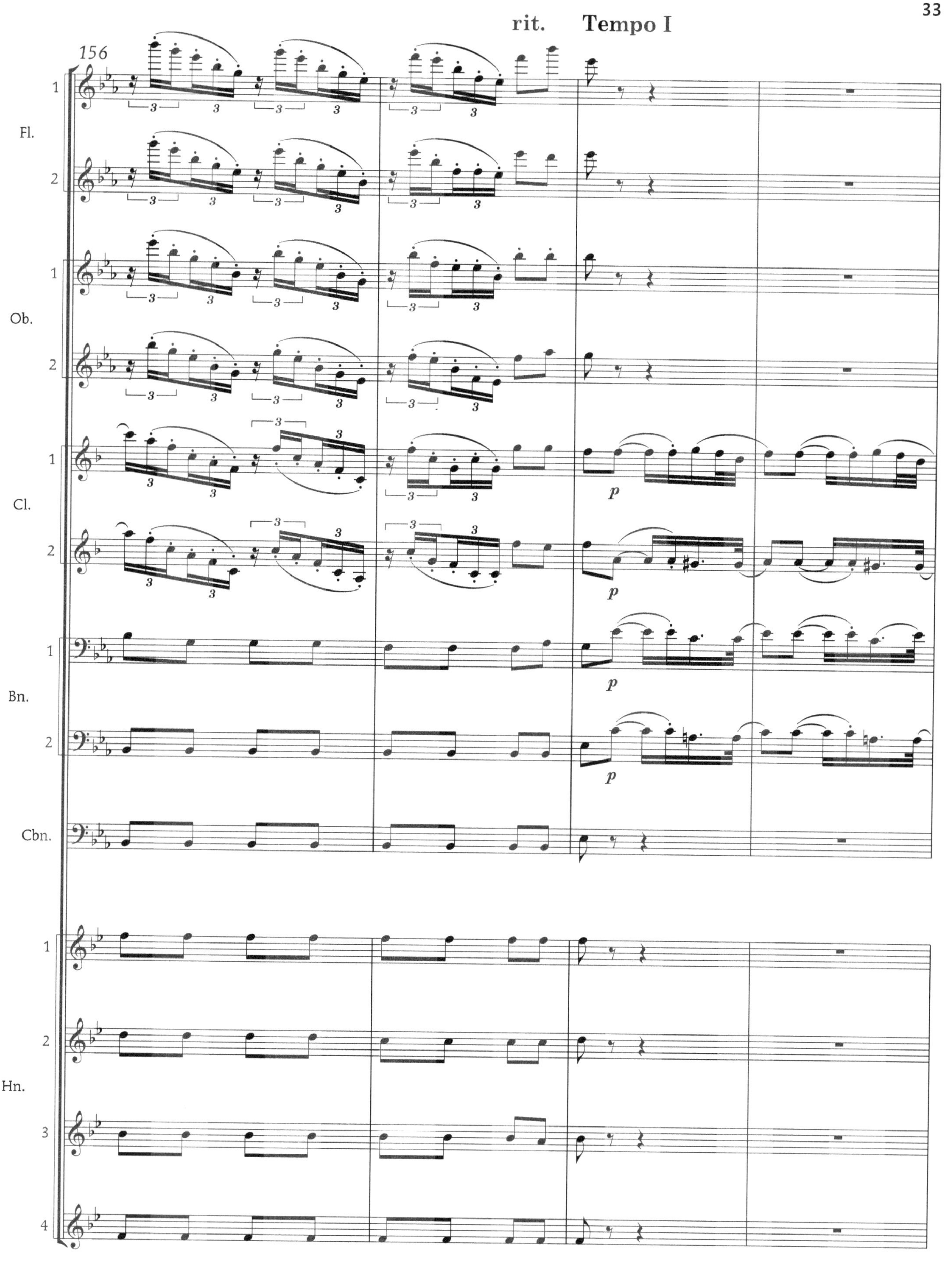
rit.
Tempo I
156
Fl.
1
2
Ob.
1
2
Cl.
1
2
p
p
Bn.
1
2
p
p
Cbn.
Hn.
1
2
3
4

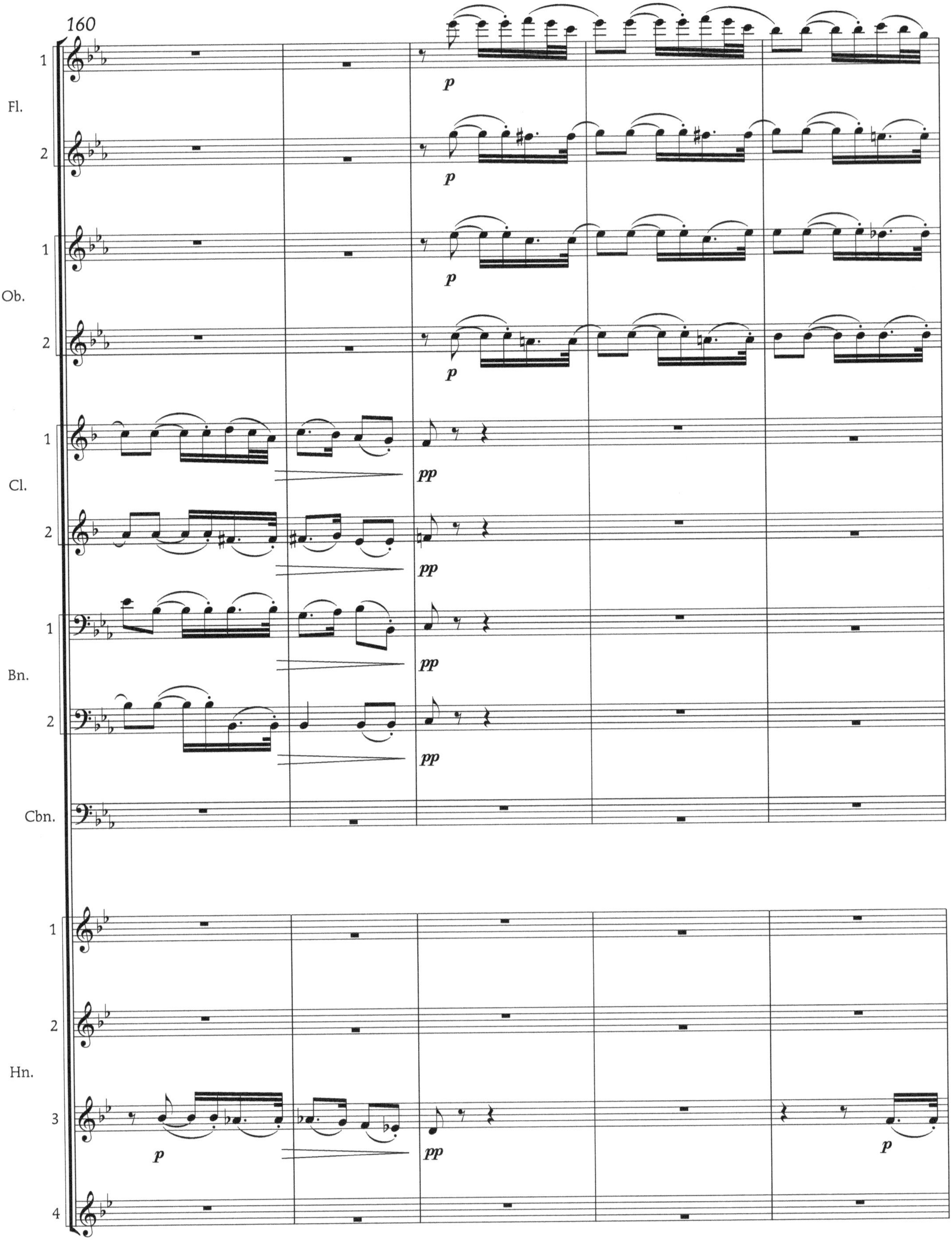
160
Fl.
1
2
Ob.
1
2
Cl.
1
2
Bn.
1
2
Cbn.
Hn.
1
2
3
4
p
pp

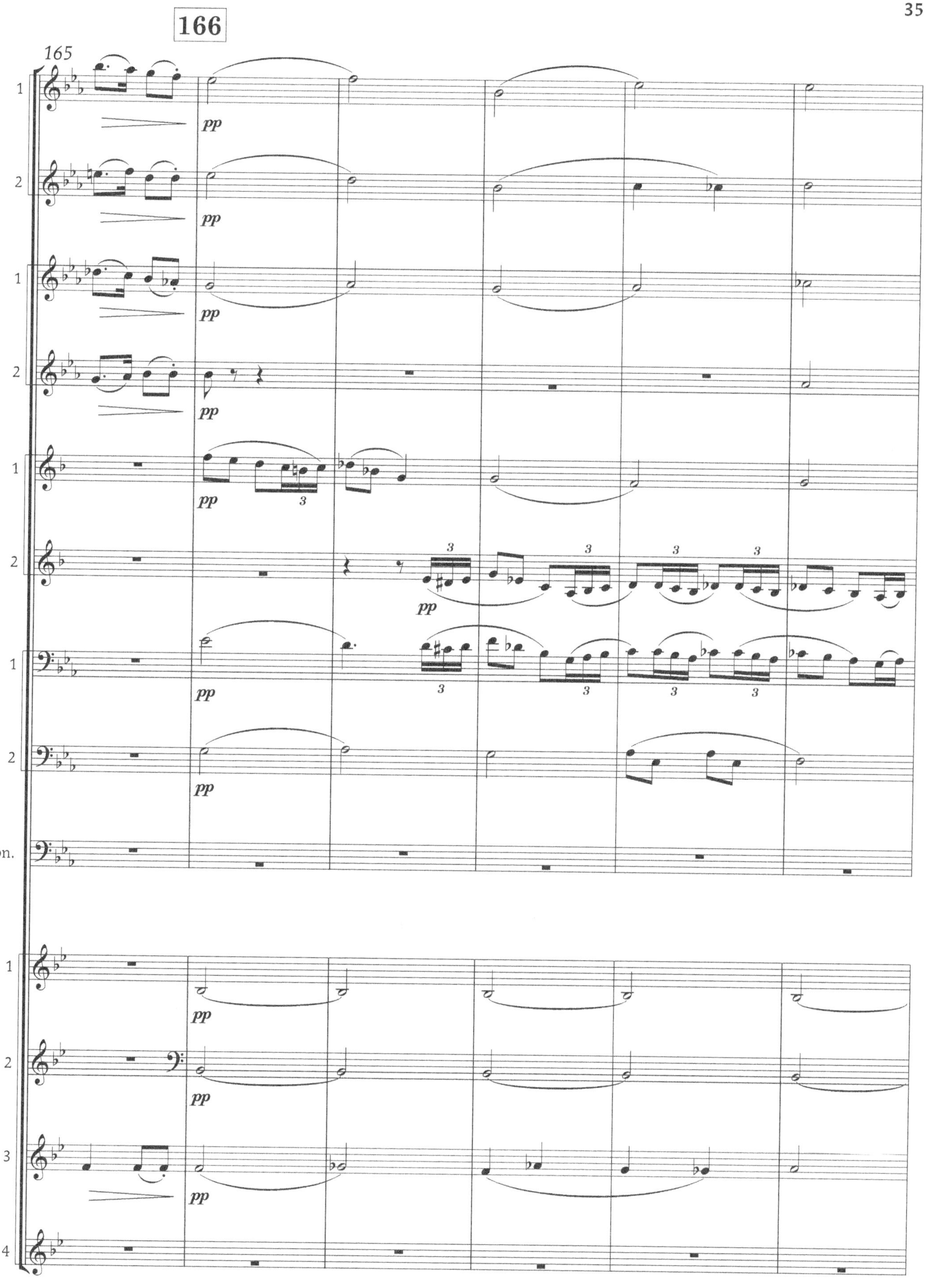
166
165
Fl.
1
2
pp
Ob.
pp
Cl.
3
pp
Bn.
3
pp
Cbn.
Hn.
1
2
3
4
pp

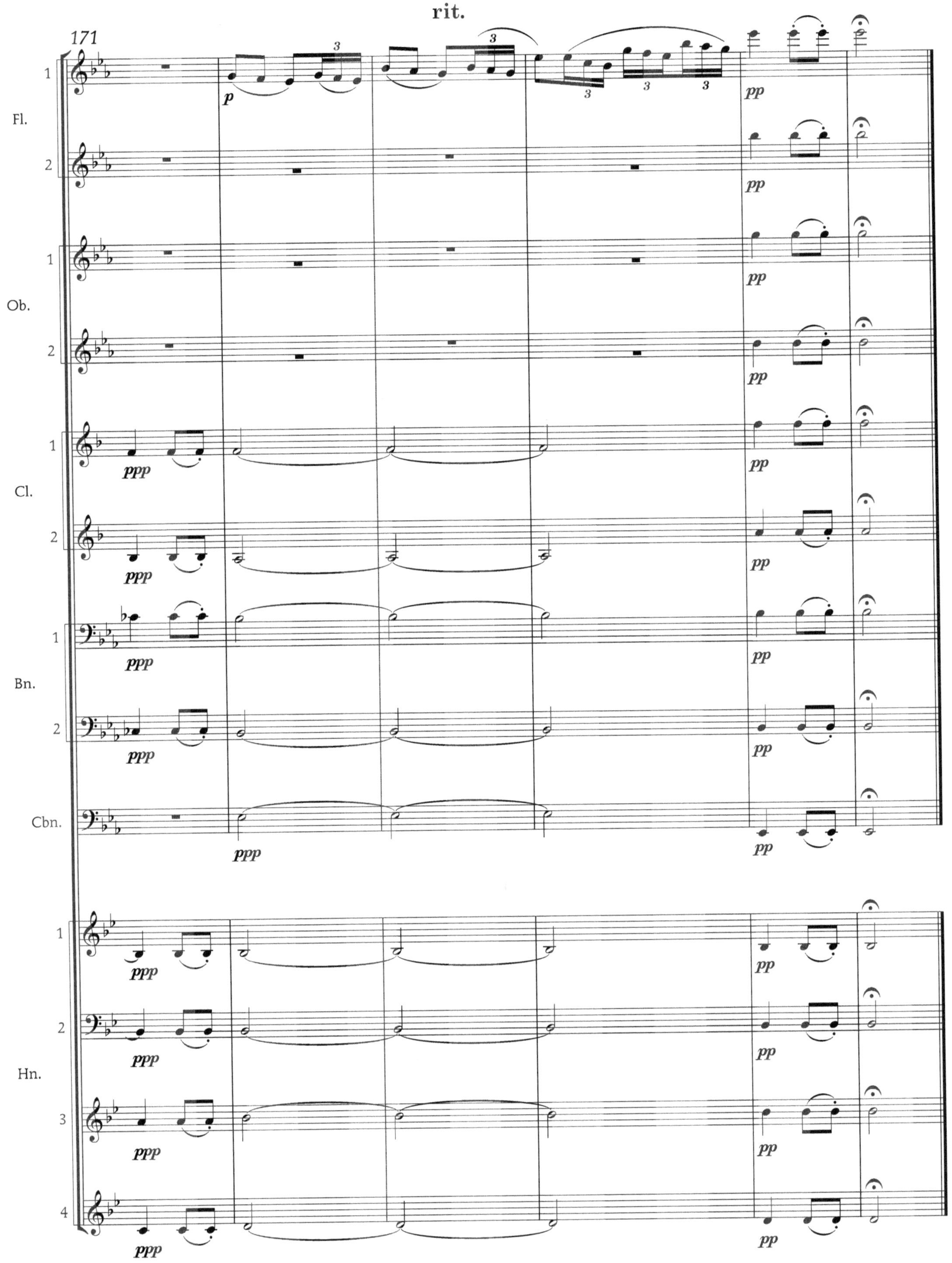
rit.
171
Fl.
Ob.
Cl.
Bn.
Cbn.
Hn.
p
pp
ppp

www.ingramcontent.com/pod-product-compliance
Lightning Source LLC
Chambersburg PA
CBHW081154040426
42445CB00015B/1887